MW00627054

GREEN BODIES

GREEN BODIES

Rosemary
Winslow

THE WORD WORKS
HILARY THAM CAPITAL COLLECTION
WASHINGTON, DC

First Edition   First Printing
Green Bodies
Copyright © 2007 by Rosemary Winslow

Reproduction of any part of this book in any form or by any means, electronic or mechanical, including photocopying, must be with permission in writing from the publisher. Address inquiries to:

The WORD WORKS
PO Box 42164
Washington, DC 20015
editor@wordworksdc.com

Cover art: *Prayer Web II* by John Winslow,
          54" x 40", oil on canvas, 2006

Book design, typography by Janice Olson

Printed by Signature Book Printing, Inc.
          www.sbpbooks.com

Library of Congress Number: 2007925637
International Standard Book Number: 0-915380-676
ISBN 13: 978-0-915380-67-1

Acknowlegments

So many to thank, all my family, friends, teachers, colleagues, who've brought me to the place where I could write these poems. Especially: Eamon Grennan, Eric Ormsby, and Baron Wormser for their long and patient encouragement and excellent critiques of poems and the arrangement of the book; teachers—Galway Kinnell, Richard Murphy, Sharon Olds, Stanley Plumly, and Barbara Sobol; the Federal Poets; Karren Alenier, Bernadette Geyer, and Judith McCombs, for helping the manuscript to become the best it could be; Janis Haswell, Mary Stevenson, Sue Thomas, and Pamela Ward; and most, my husband John, first reader and daily companion in the arts and in life. For funds and time to write and complete the manuscript, ever gratitude to the DC Commission on the Arts & Humanities for three Larry Neal Awards and a writer's grant; and the Vermont Studio Center for a residency grant. Special thanks to the editors of the following journals in which some of the poems first appeared, sometimes under slightly different titles, and some in earlier versions:

32 Poems Magazine: "Palomino"
Beltway: An Online Journal of Poetry: "Foxes," "Linden," "Backyard"
Crossroads: "When Grandfather Died"
The Federal Poets: "In Love, Approximately"
Innisfree Poetry Journal: "Beslan, Et Alia," "Blood/Wine," "Flamingos," "Mother, Then & Now," "The Day," "The Elegy," "To a Fish," "Transport," "Walking Quaker Whiteface Road I Meet My Brother"
Pinstripe Fedora: "Out"
Poemeleon: "After *The Seven Acts of Mercy*"
Poet Lore: "5 a.m.," "Driving: Night Along the Susquehanna," "Listening, Late September"
The Potomac Review: "Carnal"
The Schuykill Valley Journal: "Igloo"
The Southern Review: "Going Home"
Valparaiso Poetry Review: "Kingdom of Cloth, Three Women, a Naked Boy"
Wind in the Timothy: "City Park, Early Morning"

ANTHOLOGIES

"Going Home" is reprinted in *Voices from Frost Place, Volume II,* CavanKerry Press, 2004
"Palomino" is reprinted in *Letters to the World,* Red Hen Press, 2007
"Apricots," "Black-Eyed Susans," and "Chasm" appear in *The Why and After,* Deep Cleveland Press, 2007
"Lightweight," "Transport," "Foxes," and "Walking Quaker Whiteface Road I Meet My Brother" are reprinted in *Wonalancet Songs,* Antlers Press, 2007

RADIO READINGS

"The Dark Rustling" was read on NPR (New York)

AWARDS

The Larry Neal Awards for Poetry: First Place, 2006, for "Chele's Air," "Chele's Belvedere," and "Kingdom of Cloth, Three Women, a Naked Boy"; Second Place, 2002, for "To a Fish"; Third Place, 2001, for "5 a.m." and "Naming the Trees"

for Michael *That in black ink my love may still shine bright.*
—William Shakespeare

the iceberg cuts its facets from within . . .
—Elizabeth Bishop

Contents

⌐ 3 ⌐

Palomino

                              web of perpetual light,
      holding us so gently we don't even know, as

those summers I hung at sunrise from the sisal swing
looped and knotted to the chestnut limb parallel with
the ground and the loose dirt spilling up from my feet's
start-up pacing under my seat and settling, it took me arcing
me and time eased unimpeded by suddenness and terror,
I looked out on fields of timothy bordered by trees.

I loved those millions of stems, each one a cut of light,
and light coasting across to the shape of the wind.
I loved those thousands of hands of trees lifting and
swinging from light sturdy stems, pendulous, weighted by air,
the softer maples' sleeves, and the birches' rattle,
I hung suspended in the light gold morning light.

What can I say when I can't see light
until it casts itself to the actual flesh of things?
I try to think, but it comes to me:
I want a quieter song than I've had in my life.
I want, I want
                        And then, like agony, a stampede of dust.

Walking Quaker Whiteface Road I Meet My Brother

Yesterday a funeral, a bad X-ray,
futile the guessing—what future?
Heart turns backward, now ahead

now back again, tonight, walking the dirt road
that ends at the meetinghouse by the covered bridge
at the cemetery where the first settlers are buried,

when over the houses and pine-quilled slopes
a strange luminous fog opened around me
floating

the blue dark muscled onward
the sun not quite gone over
burning a bald rock face—bronze, red,

then amethyst, high over the thickening white—
too calm, I looked back,
a quick wind troubled my sleeves.

Once in my grief
I saw something of my brother appear
the night after the funeral

as I walked the floors of the house.
A place of whiteness, and sensed conveyance—
it is all right.

I am alright, I thought.
A president's funeral played on the TV,
pictures of boys, brothers, husbands, my own,
in jungle fatigues washed out in static.

My brother, I said, not quite aloud,
so long it had been I'd spoken his name.

♪ ♪ ♪ ♪

You were a quick throw, baseball bat
in either hand, legs lean and fast.
You worked hard, played hard,

we walked the farm hand in hand,
kicked clumps of dirt, inhaled the richness.
What is it to lose a life you never

had time to live? I wonder now,
this thing in my chest, stone, or
lapsed piece of flesh over my heart.

That last night, all you'd been through,
trying to justify your unwanted arrival,
your life, then cancer, fifteen, the end.

What did you see when you said,
Everything is so beautiful . . . beautiful . . .
that vision you had as we stood around you

waiting, praying the night would not end,
your words continued in the rhythm of our breathing,
then you said— *Do you love . . . ?*

It fell among us like an unfinished sentence.
My heart turned around on its muscle.
Right then I loved you mightily.

That is what you became.

Reddening leaves of maples falling
into the gold birches
and on to the packed dirt road,

leaves scattering like melody
coming to rest,
my whole body was pulsing.

I got there in the darkness,
passed through that light filled fog,
went through the iron gate

which leaned open on loosened hinges.
Inside the stone fence the families' hands
had laid, who lay now in perfect quiet

next to each other, I stood a long time,
the day shorn, my feet hurting.
I was going toward death, maybe.

Yet I was happy. It was almost beyond beauty,
pine-fragrant, fog swirling the stillness,
the stones leaning, writing slowly vanishing.

I stood there. I stood, wondering, a clear space.
Michael, my angel, how are you?
Emptiness overhead hurtling the stars farther.

In memoriam: Michael Kevin Landow

To a Fish

When the waters tabled out
beneath you, and the spooling cable
cranked the net upward
and set you dripping
flashing, above your world
I think you must have been afraid
more than I am now looking at you
under the kitchen lights.

Bonito, little good one,
you have already given
your life. Still
I hesitate to scrape and delve
your black eye takes me so,
your mouth open a little
as if to say whatever fish say
when they go.

I have been to the top
of one tree only—and it
was small. I have walked
along rooftops, I have not died.
You lie, half up half
down in fluorescence
all sequined shine
as once in the water's light.

I handle the knife—raise the flashing
steel above you. Now what
strange joy? so clear your dead
beauty in my hand.
One clean quick
swipe in your belly and red

redder than any red I remember
floods out of your white flesh,

waterfall over my hands,
pool on the table.
What cure? It seems to me
a Jordan. In stopped time
I see a knife
once put to me,
bone opened white to daylight,
red flood on concrete.

Fish, you've remembered me.

We live and die
by need, we live
by gift.
The body,
the breaking, the dark eye —
this too is glory.

Driving: Night Along the Susquehanna

counting the dead deer upturned where they fell
    the insides of the legs, the bellies
      white in the headlights and starless night,
I saw into the hazed past how they'd bounded on grass.

At length I came to the house
    I had never lived in,
      built later and half underground
against the cold of Buffalo's winters.

Two o'clock in the afternoon
    two hours too late
      to see him alive.
The bed stripped to its plastic sheet.

An aluminum trapeze dangled
    where he'd gripped his body up
      because he was weak,
and glinted because a small light slanted in.

At the front door, on either side of it, seven rifles leaned.
    I hadn't known he was afraid, so I think
      he died early on purpose, knowing I was coming,
him whom I feared for most of my life.

Mother was alone,
    it seemed almost night,
      so little light,
though outside May shone on the new leaves and parsley.

She had a glow I'd never seen in her,
    relief?
    calm?
We came to each other across the room.

⬛

In the first days of grief, a friend told me
    today, the body of the one left behind
    sends forth a river of calming chemicals.
A stunned comfort pervades.

And the fatally struck ones? In the very last moments
    does the clenched hand loosen? the hoof
    delicately droop? Is there peace on the road they wanted
or didn't want to cross?

"They gave him a dose," my sister raved
    when she arrived, "that's why
    he didn't last as long as the doctor
predicted. I suspect . . . "

But I couldn't listen to what she feared
    the hospice folks had done unwisely,
    I think it was too hard for him to hang on.
Or, he let go so he wouldn't have to meet me face to face.

Another starless night arrived. The three of us
    drove off to a restaurant in town. Mother
    ordered shrimp, my sister and I, lobster.
The plates arrived, pink meat on beds of kale and foiled potatoes.

She told the final episode:
    "He raved all night
        they were coming to take him away,
'Don't let them!' he screamed, but he wouldn't let me near him

    until light broke at six o'clock
        and then he slept.
        He never woke."
She repeated it several times.

Then we began to eat in the mute light,
    picking the pinkish meat delicately
    out of the fingernail-like material
the beings had been alive in yesterday.

We were a cluster, three women
    alive after a disaster,
    a tornado of a man.
But didn't speak of that.

Father-Stuff

Let's get the worst over first, you say?—
the day he went mad at Princess my cat
after she birthed five kittens on my brothers' bed.
(She must have liked their smell, the soft worn cotton.)
This was the Fourth of July. I was ten.
July Sixth. Afternoon. Sun bright as cloud-
riddled territory gets. I carried her out
in my arms, she wriggled against my chest,
my heart. I trembled, I shook, I begged, for his
rifle seesawed from his hand. You guessed it—
he did it. I cried for three days and fed
the little babies milk from doll bottles.
The worst part was he brooded on shooting himself
down by the pond. But he didn't.

Lightweight

June, too wet to plow—*if* he were here now.
I thrash between countries, dream he's okay—
tanned as July, hat brim cocked fifties' style,
riding the fields, without the suit—then he's not.

Box shouldered, I heft him up, climbing rungs.
I meet some travelers, I say—*I'm trying to love
this.* But they stop, stare, look away. I almost
make it. Next night he's back, knifes my cat.

Today a hawk kept south of Chocorua's
crest, hooked wings flat, slicing wind power.
Sun on the granite, we ate lunch where a chieftain
trapped by colonists once opened his arms
all the way down to the gorgeous valley.

When night lit down, rocking chairs groaned, the citronella
worked. Moths, drunk with poison, fought to scale
the pail's galvanized lip for light. Eating wings
the flame crackled and thrilled, as it had to,
as *I* had to—caught staring, blood kindling.

Linden

Tea of dried flower, toothed heart-shaped leaf.
Linden for soothing, grandmother would grieve,
speaking in English, to me. I used to blame

all the family's troubles on history—
German hordes tamed a bit by philosophy,
music, and linden. Yet I never saw that tree—

until once in a friend's neighborhood,
intoxicated by fragrance, I looked up—
blossoms of thick cream, fireworks, suns!

I saw my mother some kind of blind, so tired,
so many of us, my father laid out
an angry log sunk on the davenport,

me on the hearth trying to keep warm, the other
half the heart biting, wired for life.

Going Home

There is no going home
as usual
the vehicle stalls
in reverse gear
in mud tracks

as essential as
the flat fields, the blades
of shadowed pines over the drive,
the sun bleeding
from the west.

On the rise the house,
painted clapboard, the color of cream,
is rented now like bodies
of water and minerals made
living by some miracle

which is to say some process
we don't understand.
Some day we'll have a
different owner,
a different lover,

pine trees and whirling wind
that primitive communion
a new testament
of each generation.
All going home is never going back—

there may be ruin and mud tracks
deep to make wheels spin. The only way

is slogging on,
or else walking
on water.

Or yet it may be dry
the sand flying in your nostrils
but you must breathe, must go, must go
on, which is to say, go on making
required visits, like stations

of a cross. It is a way
of finding what we lost
or never had, of learning we are only
renters, and making new covenants,
going where we belong.

Backyard

at first I thought
mysterious fire
neon valentine
o! heart shape

flaming foil
through the skinned
limbs of the myrtle

but it was
the eastern sun
come to swim
a red brick wall

so now the myrtle nods
droops bunches
of deep pink clusters

over the stairwell
where I stare
into their yard

the neighbors
do not
speak to us

Trial

Is it true what we recall of what happened
is not as bad as what actually did?
We all have a talent for the painful, and
for pleasure. The mind's labor, always mixed.
Why then do so few make it out of steady numbness?
It's not as easy as childbirth, unartfully
accomplished, which you might be thinking of now.
Consider Nancy. She rests little, *tap tap tap,*
her shoes all day, trying to keep quiet while
the redbud tree outside tries to tone down
in her blue eyes, sap running to ground.
She hates winter but lives there, hauling its gown.
Not so bad, thinking she forgives them all.

Out

If I cast the knife edge of my eyes
on the waters
I can move

If I kneel down on a bank with willows
shadows lie down
like sleeping dogs

If I turn west other shadows I meet
flicker and stay
as I pass

If I look up a gull's white underside catches
and splits gold light

If I look north snow beyond eyesight
blue streaking across

Each crystalline flake different they say
hard to imagine

Where am I going from here?
stuck to my heels interminable shadow
faithful won't say

Sun ascends
snow white blinding
If I cast my knife edge on the waters I can move

In Love, Approximately

I feel days
when sun-dazzled leaves
leap to heaven
or fingertips.

My hands are in love
with proximate things.
They fly at the sun.
The blood bird sings.

Leaf-vein—my kin—
what can I do but
touch, touch . . .

I cannot reach
        heaven
                nor him

Listening, Late September

splendor of
venus appearing
over the red brown leaves
blue to blue violet arriving
slip of white eyelash
background of evening

traffic down to contralto
leaf crunch under tires
lawn edges yellow
red dress of holland
far memory
a future

deep in shadow
the insect engine ascends
calling the lovers calling again
steady preliterate willful
as the treadle my mother rocked
back and forth under her foot

as she hummed
mending one
of my father's shirts
or gathering the waist
of a new red skirt
father enters predictable

we are happy to see him
carry him coffee tell him our day
all of us children are given good supper
she is lifting her head to pray

it is so calm in the quiet
there is no fear

well—it was never like that
and if I could go back
to that time
and give it this
evening I would
go I'd go

tonight there is
blue and blue violet
white eyelash of moon
stars over the houses
it is so clear
inside the song

The Elegy

My husband is making a scene—
a ladder about to tip over, pots of paint in disarray,
and orange flames. His mother is dying.

She is not in it, she is already gone,
locked in the imbricated grays, the strewn
oils on the floors, her empty chair near the center.

And he is twenty again,
pupil and antagonist,
sprawled where her feet would be, his hands holding him upright.

The background is
the country town they summered in,
same street, same houses, same church with steeple.

The chair like the town
is nineteenth century, bygone,
a horseshoe arm rail with carved spindles.

She is not there, and if you did not know her
she cannot hold the painting together —
what you would see is emptiness, longing, and fire.

Which is what holds us together now.
He turns to my staring,
his eyes fly over me like blue gaps

to the track lights on the ceiling.
Where is she going?
Where are we *all*?

Next month he will be back at it,
regarding then moving in closer,
painting over the edges of flame.

It will look more tranquil, and sadder.
She will be gone.
He will not have finished it.

Foxes

They are alive somewhere
in the block of blackness that is trees,
the two foxes whose gold eyes
locked and gleamed as our headlights pried
nothing out of them, who waved off
through a door they opened in the grasses.

We had stopped to look at the stars.
No cloud, no moon, and the world's
electric dimming three hundred miles away.
We were looking up, your breath stirred
tendrils on my neck, your wet mouth
was atop my head, I was a grass

waving. It was our first night, you
were a stranger. Fragments
of constellations whirled, wildness
cabled down through the woods, you went
into me, I went into you, some kind of light
wheeled as we stood, we were a grass

entered. Black heaven was alive,
had reached us across immeasurable spaces.
And was there as we drove back,
and was waiting all through the days
I did not know how to love you.
You waited, and we grew like grasses.

2

Igloo

The child's body drew a circle in
the tallest drifts,
taller than she was,
with sticks from trees that were her friends
in summer, and lay impotent now
on winter ground.

She packed snow in corners
for a table and chairs
and a bed in the deepest recess
of the cave
to lay her head upon.

When she couldn't go home
because the babies were crying
and the fire was not yet made,
she built a shelter
from the wind that whipped
across her white life.

Even now she lives there.

Chasm

what   *memory*   *is this?*

                                                Gripped

wrist in her father's hand   her shocked feet   red   iced

land of snow

                   kitchen lights

                                black gape

                                         plunging

                  remember   *Remember!*

coming at her   red in the face father

                                   And far far

away mother   across across across across

        small shoes   shiny black   gripped in her hand

Sheep

flowed by   yellowy clouds
soft through trees   heads like rocking horses   down
up   down   tugging up grass   roots sticking out teeth
all around   a man-shape   kneeled   over a girl
down there   dress up   mussed up   no shoes

up in the pear tree   that girl looked down   that girl
she could see   looked like *her*   and that man   *like*
grandfather   rubbing her skin   but warm up here
in the pear   grass all around   leaves   sheep   clouds
like cream   at the top of milk jar   no hurting —

all of a sudden   shaking!   waking up in that girl   shaking
      apart!   tumbling huffing loud   her every where out
and thunder come running sky cracking thunder
them sheep flying apart tumbling away but the ram near
falling   slow crumbling   moon horns   legs sticking out

— *get out get out get out*   yelling flying rifle father
tugging tugging tugging father pants *Not him   not that*
ram   that man that man   begging the father Mad as
Sinai quaking   yelling and gun running around the trees
other man walking slow slow slow bent   toward the fence

Carnal

crumpled and blooded   she curled
under a stairwell   in hay   she didn't
smell the field smell   she lay in it
couldn't move   *a crushed cat?   dead*
she thought   now   grandfather gone
that girl   there under the stairs
couldn't move   *this is   dead*

she knew it   couldn't say it out
blooded and crushed   she slid   into
a yellow-gold slit   an eye   in haze
each stem of hay   one   another   put one
in her mouth   *how dry   how sweet*   she
knew what animals knew

simple air grew
around   as they chewed   chewed
chewed that afternoon   and   stumbled up
out   fist   mouth   full   of hay
somehow   no body   came
to save   she limped in   went through
the house door   *miraculous!*   and told

A Story

the light
       swooped
              from the ceiling

the kitchen shook
             the table cupboards
chairs   mother   *Mother!*

she babbled   she tugged
she grabbed the big skirt
       she wept

     hurting hurting!
     Here! Here!
     she clapped her
     mouth she said
      belly

     she did it
     that girl
     bit it not her!

     that man hit
     her hit her
     put that thumb thing
     hurting!

the big skirt tugged
away and scolded
     dress— mussy
     shoes—missing
     Stop—making things up!

the big skirt swirled
                over her
hair dress body
            the kitchen shook

the light would not calm down

then loops of *eeeeeeeeeeeeees*
            grew each day
            round around
                rosy water
        on white shining
            butcher paper
                that skirt
                let fall
            from meat
                to
            linoleum

            and every
        unhappy afterschool
        she wrote *eeeeeeees*
    and drew what she knew

The Gothic Truth

not making a sound   she watches the grindstone
wobbling   hung turning   him spitting   not stopping
the blade laid on it   *scrape scrape   round round
round*   made the yard bubble   like thousands of
his bees   his one hand turning the handle   his one
hand pressing the blade   *sharp shining*   on it

but *August!*   no sheep   no pigs   hanging
beheaded from the chestnut   but *here*   her
grandfather going   those hook-and-eye boots
always-brown clothes   that scratchy moustache
she followed   she could not *No!*   and pebbles
looked up   grass stems too   whispered   *stay still*

and in the garage   no car   but hammers   saws
wrenches   awls   hanging from nails in their places
and wavy light   drew down   from dirty windows
wavy boxes of shining   *oh! dirty there* concrete   He
stood in it   mouth jerking machine   Spoke
Don't tell ever again Never Never Never say No

prick in her neck   made her look down at near
a girl near losing her head   But *wait!*
    she wasn't   she might   that arm
his hand   was pulling   was straight   was
    blooding   was *white!   bone! like animals*
inside her   *too!*   and strings of muscle   *meat!*

the eyes saw it all   no word came out   couldn't
scream couldn't get up   head buzzed   and cold
hard cold   she felt it black   big   bigger than her
and hating!   and somewhere put it   near
the weeping blood like the statue of Jesus in church
safe in a box   (not telling)   ticking

Crocodile

> *like them*
she wanted to swim
like the boys, they
paddled out far
leapt in the sunned on water
shouted with sun
squinting she watched them

> *like them*
she wanted to swim
she puddled bent-legged
on all fours
alone on the edge
squish-fingers in mud
squint-eyes looking

> *like them*
she was in the water
but there was
that white tape
stuck on that gauze

over ointment
that *slice*
in there scared her
down to bone

and the orders
keep that elbow out
she knew—of pond,
washbasin,   rain

half that warm summer
wondering *what*

was in there
in her heart

          like them
she was making up games
tracking monsters
waiting
with slit eyes
thick green hide

half-above water
long jaws a hundred sharp teeth
dark wound
powerful tail

while out there
leaping crashing
whole bodies
half that warm summer

then after
claws
long jaws
a hundred teeth inside her

Apricots

When too many hurts backed up
in that house confusion rained—
angers, hatreds, terrors plunged
from hands, mouths, furniture—
they said, *Don't make trouble,*
Stop making things up.
Little hands went up to the mouth
but it didn't stop. And then
they sent her away.

In the *other* house,
things stayed put.
A big coal stove squatted
solid and steady beside her,
it warmed her listening
to hymns and tunes flying up
from cousins hands rippling
song she couldn't see and
the rippling lines in the brown
wood of the piano stayed put,
the furnace sat warm beside her
and all the while
aunt and uncle moved
like B flats about the rooms.
And when they were away
a tall clock kept the hours,
she sat there in the quiet
between chimes
in the solid room
trying to play the keys.

Outside the apricot tree stood
silent in stripped branches

while suns and moons passed through.
And when the buds arrived
she wondered if the little red arrows
hurt the limbs. And then the small green
roundnesses and waiting and
waiting for the yellow-orange
fruit. She wasn't allowed to pick
it. But some fell down in their ripest days,
she gathered those up
in a glass bowl on the dresser,
ate them in the darkness
just before sleep.

In winters, when she was there
and warmed by the coal stove,
she stole down to the cellar
just to look at them. In the half-light,
the rows of bright jarred globes
seemed an entire universe.
Her fingers choired over the rounded
glass, went to her opened lips,
her eyes opened rounder, darker—
there, a language of fire, mute, sweet, kept—
a way to sing what she knew,
to continue.

When Grandfather Died

she cried, *You*
are too true,
my life

drips like gold
honey globes
from white

hexagonal cells. It soaks
this chunk of bread. Hard and sweet.
And she would not eat.

Rain was all through April, dew, tasteless, clear,
washing death from the bedroom, the scent of him.
The pale wallpaper was slipping down.

Carnelian hollyhocks grew a fence of six-foot pikes
around the house. His thrilled bees tore
the liquid from their blond throats. She wouldn't speak.

She put salvia in her hair, roses and peonies
in crystal vases, old beer steins, anything
that he had loved. The empty place

(Once the barn, some calves, his horses
gone in a fire
sank to spilled black stars)

became a melt
of white-pink phlox
behind the house beyond the fence. She flooded

all the rooms with flowers
till bees buzzed about our ears
far into the evenings in the parlor. She let

the clicking pendulum, his violin,
saturate the night. She would say
nothing, nor weep. And heavy afternoons spread tendrils

wet on her neck, water clung
brackish in the steins. Fruit rotted. Then
the frost came. One morning

we found her, a winter stem,
cold and stiff in the bed where he left
her. We spent Christmas snowed in,

watching the moon put a glaze on
the thick drifts,
as we'd watched her,

memory's fatal light,
that cold diffusion
distilling as we looked and looked

and could not reach her.

Black-Eyed Susans

they talked   to her
she heard

strips of wild   between the dusty
lane & field

mettle middle muddle   eye-brown
hold   rayed

petals (blank bright yellow rhymed) little
sun-glow

knew not distant
daze

she kept them   hidden in
finger curl   of brain

minding how the bruising came
became world

time   again-summer sun-praised world
against again

skin-fist   dull-eye   no-mind   flare-brown
animal-freeze   spun-gold

petals said   *it's all right   night fills
every center*

I live   you keep on living
and she did

and soon forgot
they were

but they were   and held
the bruised world

away from her

Apples

oh how she loved them!   sharp green
sauce   pie   anything made of them

one bite couldn't hurt   *yet wait wait*
for the soft yellow ripen   sang to her

and some whispering *can't hurt   can't hurt*
one taste   one bite   —   just one

hard bite   sharp juice   awed dark mouth
sudden whole world   When out of

Where?   *stomachache stomachache*
shouting   hitting   cheek   skull   fall

limp grass around   green pants
his shoes mudded   at her eyes

salt-taste drip   lip   nose   cheek
stinging banging blossoming out

                in the world of love for him
salt-stone   sword-fire   split-man

starry swimming head   in the world
of love for him   for one bite   one

Seventeen

                                           At last
she fit   into the orange sweater   the one
the neighbor gave   the one her father
had an eye for   And the others were away

                                           Now
the guitar   the deep waist   her breast fit there
she played she leaned   into learning   strumming
her left hand finding the chords   And he

                                        Liked
it there   new and round   he stared and stared
narrowed eyes   jittering burning   but she doesn't
see him she is learning   when   *Upstairs*

                                     Take it
off seething   She flew off Up where nothing
hid her   not curtains shades blankets other
clothes or bodies she could shed   shelling

                                     Speed-
ing sleeves faces selves bras fast speeding But
the eyes black coal came burning through
the hand came burning thrumming   spill-

                                     ing
fire   melting flaming   her to light   stealing
her steeling white   her new round   her face flying
iced sheet   cheek   voice   flying to

                                     Pieces

Four Five Six . . .

she slid into the cold kingdom
behind the blue curtain
clump clump clump clump
his boots coming

she began —
one two
unbuckle the shoe
three four
open the door

and she did
and he did

his heaviness
against her

five six pick
up the stick
seven eight
lay it straight

and she did
and he did

smoke in the room
kerosene that smell

seven eight
open the gate

and she did
she flew without wings
under the stairs
an alcove
honeycombs he kept there

his thumping thighs erased

      ■

the first time
she thought she'd died
the wet red way
her body lay
in ruin

and they said   *don't cry*
     they said   *don't make trouble*
     they said   *don't lie*

she was a hurricane without an eye

one two buckle the shoes
three four shut the door
five six pick up the sticks
seven eight lay them straight

and she did   she drew
and drew and drew and drew
in sand ground fine
by wheels animals tools
at the foot of a little hill

she gave her time to
stared and stared
at a black hole
nine ten do it again
forgetting it almost
all

      ■

some say it is
impossible to forget

and they are correct

she didn't
and they didn't

take no thought
she heard from the pulpit
sufficient unto to the day
is the evil
see no evil
hear no evil

she was a hurricane without an eye

she was a flower a snow bank an acorn a bride

　　　　▪

one two buckle my shoe
three four shut the door
five six she prayed and prayed
seven eight for heaven's gate
nine ten　　nine ten
the old man went
then
her father turned
toward her
her mother turned
away

nine ten
do it again

nine ten
do it again

3

5 a.m.

I rise from a wreckage of sleep
again the long blind scarf of grief

and yesterday and yesterday's
gunmetal page

the porch lights hiss
at the shroud-hung sky

I go down the stairs to the garden
to be where the roses are leaning

heavy and sweet on the long fence
I lift my face from burial

into burial in the softness of flowers
that is like the skin under the necks of animals

tears shine
in the small white crosses

in their fire centers
the star clematis has made

and entered on
the dead espaliered pear

suddenly I am
jarred

wheep and again
wheep wheep I hear

hidden birds
coming alive

one by one
in the trees

thick pollen of light
undraping the roof lines

composing the sky

The Dark Rustling

eastward   striding the pines
in giant

taffeta gown
suddenly

        leapt
into body

white-dappled gentleness:
fawn

in the diffused sphere
porch light thrown

black nose   near our feet
we dared

not move   we gazed back only
wet mud-brown eyes   stricken

seeking some   *what?*

forming   not forming
but there   alive   seeking

       ◾

your face letting it in
letting it out

three   three   us
how many minutes? I

could have counted time
on my fingers

but we were
edgeless

I had no clue
to reach out

where she stood
on her delicate hoofs

rose up on four stalks
into creature

sudden flower of meat   *yes*
as we were

so I did not
you did not

move a micron from our stations
but when she turned

her black nose upward
and turned her length into a U

whipped back eastward
returned to pure amplification

—do you remember?
that taste of wonder

love's tongue wanting *more*—

it was then the sharp barking cones
funneled the air

                                    —*coyotes!*
a pack out of night earth

all night we tangled arms
in light sleep

knives shining
images of body   her   above us

                    ◾

in the morning
we walked out toward sunrise

stepping on blades
of soft light

walking on feet more
in their flesh than ever they were

toward where the sound
had come from the night before

cracking bark and needles mingling
with hermit thrush and jay

the woods floor
littered with bear scat

and ground squirrel whimpering
cries

springing and shriveling our feet away
we were without names

we found no scraps of hide
no soft nose or eye or rib or cold leg

no neck we might have hung on if we'd dared
that night

∎

I could have melted sheer away
I counted

four bone-columns in your hand
in mine

I felt heart in bone-case
beat time forward

then away
then you murmured

let's go back
but the wet edge of sound

tumbled
from a stone-broken river

crossing the riven air

Chele's Belvedere

The last of summer, the grand world left outside, we sat down.
A low sun slid away, sky light pearled, grayed, faded.
Then the screens disappeared, the roof, the stripped bones.
Then, table, plates, a floating corner of brie.

Conversation eased, ascended, dispersed.
The parrot and his perch burned out, silent.
Yet you set no artificial light going
so the pond became an enormous bowl

in the woods black turning where a round moon
cruised low and sculled gold on the mirror
below our tumbling talk. It was the last night,
it was every night. We didn't touch. I thought how

Keats found autumn drowsed in a sun-pinked furrow,
on a chaff-strewn granary floor, a wind lifting her hair,
drifting toward cold, which never arrives in the poem.
You said, *it's as if this comes to me alone . . .*

A line of shoulders backed with light . . . no face . . .
At once pieces of darkness appeared, expanded.
Everything slipped down to beautiful quieted silt.
I thought, it would be fine to die here . . .

I felt the ease, a loosening, letting go the body . . .
You would stay here, I would go.
Everything seemed complete. What was left? . . .
The fade back before all the selves filled in.

Portrait of My Father, circa 1945

The eyes qualm: in a sea of sepia and khaki,
islands hand-tinted a pale sky, drawing backward
to cloud dream, some instinct to withdraw.
A visor shields his brow, the smile retreats
wary, a slight boat passing. The body tries
to form to the proud cloth — it fails. A sadness
uncovered — but he's one of the important
there. If no other time, ever in his
life, right now he is someone — held.

This man, so young, seemed a stranger those years
this picture kept a small table in the house.
Between his sullenness, rages, and ice,
I'd hear him singing of ecstatic Paris,
a buoyed hero striding the ocean of intense
French. Those times, his eyes were blue forests,
I couldn't see what he saw, and what he saw
had left. He hovered, apart, unsubstanced,
while the real man looked out, his eyes like inflamed scars.

Mother, Then & Now

I

I see her perfect open lips
moving through a song
standing over the kitchen sink,
a steady ping of whey
from a bag where cheese is being made
keeps perpetual time in a shiny pot
on a white stove under a wooden drying rack.
I see me drying dishes, singing along,
her thick hands in gray suds, her hair drowsed.
As always she is elsewhere and
meat for supper burns in an iron skillet.
Smoke piles up in the room.

Sometimes it was "Clementine,"
but "Abide with Me" and "Nearer
My God to Thee" were her favorites.
It didn't seem strange to me
to want heaven
instead of the life we lived.

Evenings she would sit under a lamp
with a broom length stem
and a bleary yellow shade.
A tiny needle was in her hand
weaving threads over a hole
in one of our socks. She was
so tired her head kept drifting
toward her breasts like a stuck record.
In another part of the room father
quieted finally and snored
while the TV blared
then fuzzed out to a wad of cotton.

One time (was I eight, thirteen, ten?)
I watched her descending the stairs
in a black chiffon dress, hemmed in
by shadows and plain plaster walls.
Her skirt splayed out from the belt,
umbrellaed the narrow passageway.
Her hair—I remember so well—
was arranged as in the drawings
father made on scraps of paper
and scattered about the house,
loose generous ripples falling about
his ideal womanly curves,
the bright red lips too full to be real.

And yet I never saw him kiss her,
or I can't recall, but when she bent
to kiss me that time, I was transfixed
by the transparent sleeves
over the skin of those kitchen arms
turned all of a sudden to smoky
magic. A scent of spices
trailed her, stranger
than pies, and her lips'
good night good bye to my cheek
had the astonishment of blood on snow,
so warm they were and bright,
and her eyes up close were large, they had
a sadness deeper than I could fathom then,
encompassing and vague like the fabric
where it drifted across my arms,
and father pacing across the worn linoleum
like a cat wound up between us and the door,
darting looks at the clock.

II

Outside a fit of wind
blows the maple and Queen Anne Cherry leaves,
flying up their pale undersides.
In the kitchen and over her bed
pale wallpaper is slipping down.
I watch her fitful rest, the red-orange
flowers on the paper are bridges
of the air, curling down
over her faded hair, and the brain
stricken and spilling the family secrets.

I lie down next to her, on the bed
she tells me he bought for them, he brought
her here *after the honeymoon*, she says
it as if she loved him then,
he brought her here, to *this* house
with the .22 caliber gun notched by
the door, the house her father-in-law
built, whose house this was, by law,
but not the bride, who wasn't his,
though he tried to take her.
And her husband my father
loved her but soon determined
he'd rather have married her sister
with the *pendulous breasts* (I remember this)
or else the neighbor with perpetually red
lips, waved hair, and the wrong religion.

And then she watched (this part
I add, I know) her children scattering
elsewhere away like her
in darkened corridors.

And other
things happened to her
and some to me
and some the same, it seems
a gulf across the room,
my feet careful
as if the floor
might fall,
her cheek like gauze,
my hand there,
my mother, her sadness
sinking, wringing
my own face—
How young and beautiful she was!
How she is going away from me forever.

After *The Seven Acts of Mercy*

This   This,   we want, she thinks,
desperate, ignorant, thinking
the beating heart will break, believing
it will break us, believing
it is it— not that we are still
to be found under the breastbone of the beloved.

Arriving in our darkness,
salve syllables over the winding sheet,
behind the eyes,
a dream of angels walking the stair,
or tumbling through cloud,
carries us with them,
past commiseration,
and the heart beats mightily
in the crickets' summons,

after the imperious sun,
when the slide of light breaks open the attention
and we are taken out of ourselves,
past the careful stigmata,
to a lake where a red girl in a hammock
stitches words from wreckage
under two maples, unmerited, under the hold of heaven

and she stops, quickened by an absence
of language: buttercups in the warm grass,
the *twick twick twick* of a goldfinch,
a crow's blue black, a timbre of leaves—
then remembers the torch-lit street,
its chiaroscuro of beggars and rich men's sleeves
in the stunned eyes of a young woman

giving her breast to her jailed father
under the smile of Caravaggio's Christ.

Light of night, light that folds out
from her, and on her, falling
from the smiling calm, mother and child
above, torch light thrown in flame-shape
down her face, throat, breast
where the green dress is parted—
deep heart
caught by the painter in all time

where we walk every day and do not notice
the rich the poor the quiet lake
the goldfinch the grass, afraid to walk in splendor

unless turning from time to time
to each other in acts of love
almost unendurable—
for we are not done, we darkly, hardly
able to come where no love is
and love's force insistent—*soft   here   now* —
while all around us furious joy is gathering the kingdoms.

Naming the Trees

My father knew the names of all the trees
that grew on our farm and all around
he said and he showed me how to read
by bark and leaf what was apple
what oak cherry black walnut
butternut pine spruce poplar elm ash

When I was older I learned he was wrong
about some names of flowers but never trees
I guess he had to know I knew he knew
or maybe he got it wrong from *his* father
and so on . . . it was like that at home
you could never tell what was true

Even the weeds had names that got mixed up
fire plant was red eye
soap flower got called phlox
lambs quarter was ragweed
and ragweed is something I still don't know
no one cared what folks elsewhere thought
it made a kind of mixed up sense
we lived by

Only the quince I can't now remember
though I feel even now the difficult bite
the hard tang in my mouth
I read once it was the golden apple
and the fruit that caught Eve's eye
and Adam not having named it
was put out his pride hurt and ashamed of that
I like to imagine picking one and eating it
with that in mind
how we must fall one way or another

But milkweed was milkweed
I loved the liquid white
when I broke it in my hands
it seemed both human and not
a kindred blood—determined yet innocent
scattered in corn fields and patches of dirt
uncontainable like Christ

I moved south a while back
and there are still some I don't know
four dogwoods border my yard
a neighbor's myrtle rambles
over my stairwell I like it there
bare skin and fragrant with pink
past that a cedar blocks the view
of all downtown but in winter
it cheers me up all that green towering life

Over the other fence a waxy magnolia
lazes and feels at home
and a spiral willow and a fig
my Brazilian friend smuggled in as sticks
the bamboo I recognize from the fishing poles
my grandfather loved and walloped me hard
for breaking once when I tripped in a stony field

It was never clear why this was loved
and that was not—I'm glad I'm here
where names don't have a personal past
trees are just trees a bit of nature
set with deliberation a green refuge
for the birds of the air and all of us
just to look on when we're tired out

Sometimes I sit out here and think
about things how my father made trees
feel ours—mined taken in eaten—
I think about him how his life was
how he stays in me loving the earth
how what he did was done in pain
and trees scatter around these wild things

It took me years to realize the name
ailanthus in books was the wild tree
I pulled up every summer from my garden
it grows everywhere it can find a place—
cracks in sidewalks empty lots
there are even three dug in in the rooftop mortar
of a boarded up townhouse down the block
they brighten the city (they do)
those long shapely ladders of leaves
we call it the tree of heaven

Transport

Without visible wings
pearled the
hummingbird suspends
at flower's nipple
and her heart beats mightily
as she draws the nectar up
the artery of her strange mouth

This is the way I watch her
every morning coming and going
from five to eight
it must be the same one
I've read they're so pugnacious

Her mate flies in a wide arc
up to a twig in the pine
and waits for her
his head a miniature sun
on the branch's horizon

still as night I sit near the laurel
along the porch I look and look
past the house wall past him
into the dark sensation of woods
I see nothing

more alive
than this
pure desire
for sweetness
their

electric humming
as they stand in air—
everything
they want
is now

they are so filled
when he comes down to her
their green bodies
two shimmering leaves
soft fire

then flash
over the briars
disappear—
every morning all
disappear
return

City Park, Early Morning

light exponential planking the streets
the tulips' blue throats
closed up in their cups
nodding *yes yes* to the breeze

the grass so cool
the quiet so empty
on the bench in the fragrance
of tiny white stars of clematis

now the man in the blue jacket on time
scattering bread to the starlings and pigeons
now a woman shuffling the concrete

I look up at her tumbled face and tangled hair
how heavy the cart of belongings she draws
how black the building's glass
where the tulips are nodding and nodding

Beslan, Et Alia

I cannot see it, but I see it. Stepping
Out on the porch tonight I hold
The silvered skin of the half-moon's
Waking in my palm. It has no feeling.

Nature is Innocent, and comforted
Even the woman terrorist last night
Who belted explosives over her
Womb as her hand fondled the cord

In the lamb-white diaphanous light.
A milk-tooth gnaws westward
Across faint stars from Beslan,
Children with flowers in hands

Under the thronging bells,
Shrapneled and stilled.
They will be strewn with flowers
In the bright September air.

They will not breathe it any more
Nor talk nor eat nor skip nor wake.
And there will be more.
Do not tell me not to mourn:

The world dwells in unschooled
Silver. Sleepless feet rake
Planks, bare where the first
Bronze leaf falls crushes

Upward.
                    —*How many gone?*
Safe, home, I wait for news,
Dread the light.

September 4, 2004

Flamingos

Their instincts wholly bloom
And they rise.

—James Dickey

They look ridiculous, lascivious coral
unsnowed on wet Northern lawns.
Or, righted, astride over the daffodils,
going nowhere on dulled aluminum poles.

When my sister married (the first time) she
staved dozens around the little backyard pond.
Champagne flowed, the groom got drunk, that night
in the suite's cruel privacy, he injured her.

She stayed seven livid years.   Today
in her red mustang convertible
we drive to see them live. Thousands
flow around cerulean water under the pure

zoo sky, thin stems stepping across wet sand
the brilliant bodies a cloud blossoming, and
now a burst, a flare, a pair
of black-rimmed wings fanning aslant in air.

Now, another. But someone has cut
strategic feathers, they vector, veer, fall
back next to each other, circle, squawk, settle.
No heaven here : my mind   her gaze : *I want   I wish*

Watching Elephants on Television

Here is patience—the rippling flag-
like edges of café table-size ears
they toss, casual as curtains,
listening as they chew, branches
they have pulled down and broken
between four molars, which are large as four
trunk stumps, imperturbable, a mass
of sun-dipped leaves.

Amber grasses. Sheets of light. Cooling mud at a ghost lake.
There are no commercials, there is Africa,
Iraq on another channel—fire and sand—
a president's funeral. A wand's fare
of movies, reruns, and shopping. Now they are going some-
        where,
their ears are flying, fluttering, flowering
atop the lumbering bodies,
they close in around the baby
who looks funny, a thick stump where a nose was
ripped away in an attack.
They love him, they keep him in the formidable
crowd of legs.

Now they stop,   *What is it?*   Delicate
ears wing out, sails, a fleet of them, they are
catching a sound below our capacity:
some of their kind are calling them — *Come!*
The sky hinges on a horizon.
They come up on a scrabble of bones.

Rhythm of noses long as arms, like arms,
caress of pieces – skull, vertebra, thigh –
they lift them, like silent music, they

heft, remember, ask, *What is it?* odor
of past, future, now, *they know their kind:*
They set them down like fragile
glass.

                Come   Come! — must be calling,
they move on like sea-waves, like boats on earth,
the old male in the middle, flanked
from harm by the powerful males
who minutes ago raged
up dust in a stopped blizzard of surfing,
tons of muscle, ivory crescents
of tusks, the great bodies plunged,
head to head, a great din down
through earth, a trumpeting at heaven.
The female waited on an arc of earth,
she watched with one slate eye.
When the battle was over, when she and he
had done what they knew to do, they turned back
to the herd, grazing the branches, rippling their ears.

Now it is ending, as things do—the film cuts
to prized intricate carvings and Steinways.
The News has the Avenue primed for the riderless horse.
Outside heaven tumbles down the vertical glass.

All day, through the city, rain.

Washington, DC, June 11, 2004

Kingdom of Cloth, Three Women, a Naked Boy

Beautiful the light washing him
as he lies, rich-dark as loam
on the rough cloth, as if the strong
sun of Africa exalts this one
who sleeps with a smile of heaven.

Three women hold his head,
his arms. They are covered in
rough cloth, the same rough cloth
spread under him. It is the color
of bleached wheat, of uncut canvas.

What are they doing? Who are they?
Three windows in their burkas
reveal their eyes, creased — with age?
Some rite of passage? A sign? —
The dead were sewn into shrouds . . .

No, I say, no — this boy almost a man,
perfect of face, limb, the two ladders
of ribs — ineffable peace — ten fingers,
ten toes. Two sperm pockets, limp penis . . .

The first time I held my own child,
I counted, relieved, all the perfections.
A world to ourselves. What do they see?
his loveliness? their love? famine's
exactions . . . the cloth about to close . . .

Somalia, 1993

Alone in a Strange Town

Showered gold,
pixilated disc at the ankles
of a young maple
on bleak grass outside the cold hotel.
I lean out a seventh story window, elbows in stucco,
eyeing some small black birds.
They congregate from every direction,
kaleidoscope black on white:
long-tailed V, rhizome,
fragment of abacus, crazy figure
eight. They change too fast to count
and I don't know why I want to.
Isn't the day prepared?
Paper, pencil, computer,
restless thinking so much to do
and all in a windowless room.
Now one, two, three, four,
up to thirteen, they settle, churn up, sink down
in the top twigs of the tree.
The twigs waver and still.

Insouciant tree, O spacious morning, down over the sill,
upward arising, sluicing, pestering,
something will not be lulled.

The Day

And so I came to the day
after the spring
of loving my mother
after the summer
of letting her go
under the limber pines
I lay on my back
arms stretching out
over me over the house
holding me to the blue sky
soft
how the green
melted and spread
over me and settled
fluid   mobile
the tight upraised
shoulders of my childhood
let loose their protection
settled
as the tense bands of
muscles had let go
in the spring
from against my
mother
and I had loved her then
without harm without wanting
her to be
anything she was not
and I was hardly noticeable
the movement of air barely touched
the ribbons of planks beneath me
and the blue-green tufted needles above

I was large   rich
I was gone

And not for awhile did I
rise up,
walk in the day.

Blood/ Wine

1

Drink. Changes. Love's mouth. Nuzzle and nub
of protection, after the workmen cut
the gas lines by mistake, weeks after the terror.
From a high window, I saw them pour —
out of the dormitory, their arms waving
like motherless trees, in the disaster
that might yet be. They were together
and laughing. They aimed for the corner bar.

On my way home, I saw them lounging the bar,
laughing, talking, merlot, cheap whites, ale, spilling
on chins and sweaters, communion of gladness
as they waited, not eagerly, to go back where
they live, living in cells, where they learn and learn
and are not yet very much afraid.

2

Not very much afraid, the disaster canceled,
I went down into the metro to go home.
We railed up above ground on tracks over-
hanging the city. We stopped for no reason
we knew of, for an hour we sat in the train,
night coming down, lamps lighting up, dimming
the houses. We waited and joked and told stories.
We almost slipped by the next station,

the desolate platform, the washed down concrete,
we barely slowed down—we wouldn't have known
except for the news, how while we had waited
and laughed uneasily, a desolate
red streaming dress, its heaviness,
was lifted gently (yes gently) onto a gurney.

3

Eleven o'clock news—suicide on a gurney,
counted to Christmas depression. Dis-
counted, ill-fitting pair of shoes nobody
wants to put on. Irrational— out
over the edge, quick charge of the live
track, and each viewer a witness,
each survivor an heir
to the knowledge of quick flash out.

How easy is it to feel that flame
the TV's rumoring wind fanned to ash
the very next second in the slick icicle commercial?
Did she wear a necklace? A lost
lover's heart? A cross? An initial?
Suitcase of grief riding with her over the rail?

4

Suitcase of grief, quick fix over the rail
of the bar, latched by sparkling ice, a flash
of insight arrives in the negative
everlasting comma of night, spindled
as X-ray, sheer bone left visible, grave
half-life, ending's medicine crossing
the brain's speeding life—

every one writes in the Book of Pain.
Each page opens onto the next person's.
Terror makes its marks in innocence
harshed out in Xes, crossed paradisal swords.
You can't go back. Grief's cell is cramped. Stone angels
stand at the door. Pages bleed into others. Changes.
Open the book. This is the body. Drink.

5

Drink in flood-tide, one sinks, or survives.
Listen. The stringent sibilance calls you.
What will you do? Do you think it desires you
alone? Every moment the door stands open.
Every moment any one can walk through
and meet the others. Each a particular of sorrow.
By repetitions of division the cell grows.
Root, dicotyledon, leaf, then bracted flower.
Strength comes in numbers, adage's
eternal witness, thread through ages.
But look. They are walking as *we* walk,
leaning on staffs or arms, taking the leaned
to the pool of freedom. It may be a bar,
a bedroom, a temple. Stirred, ready to enter.

6

Stirred. That's how we entered the red flowers,
rose fragrance, to glide together
on tree-shined water, two with oars,
face to face, one direction, sharing power,
love bound. The clenched hand loosens, offers
its salty palm. It wants to let go, the suffered
taste. She. He. Brachiate, it opens.
They drift through white lotuses,
afternoon light sifts through motes and mosses,
swims, rests, swims, rests, on white saucers.
A hand lingers over boat-edge, another,
water like skin, smooth satin, edge of the world.
Lovely to move toward evening, a fire,
a roof, a soft bed, a lover's promise, solaced home.

7

Solaced home, to feel the water's skin, *our* skin,
an amazing thing, to live, forgiving it all.
Disembodied saxophone moan in the next
building grounds my being. I am here.

I don't like to think nothing will become
of me when I die. Concrete mausoleum,
its secret of satin, a slow waste, the hot
unpyred commercial fire too homely.

I think I'd like to be laid out in the good
earth, in my faded blue sweatshirt and jeans,
in a pasture under a good tree—an apple—
to feed what I love. As for the remainder
of me, whatever that is, if, may it
nuzzle at love's mouth. Drink. Be changed.

Chele's Air

Up to their necks in water parabolas, two beavers pause,
slide, pause, slide, skaters, *waltzers,* across sun-wash
flashing on green shine, before *us,* watchers beside your house
step up to the muck-pocked shore, close in on magic,
this unworldly world circled by maples, pines, birches,
up-swelled air awhir with chattering, scuttling, *tu-whirps* —
our senses condensed as sniffing quietly oranges or cliffs
of snow northwind kissed to packed crystal turning
and nearing their shrink-death — spring —   star-ice of
memory, glide on, on, *on,* without freedom or choice,
what lives? Unless trail-pock of paw and cloven prints
draws us on, on, *far off* the road-cleaves . . . oh now,
the beaver in front turns, draws backward gliding, and fits
his black nose wet to his mate's — startled, suddenly, *bliss* —

For Chele

About the Author

ROSEMARY WINSLOW is on the faculty of the Catholic University of America, where she teaches writing and literature, and where she has directed writing programs for 19 years. She has published poems in numerous literary magazines and anthologies. Her scholarly work includes journal and encyclopedia articles, as well as book chapters on such subjects as Whitman, modern poets, and teaching poetry in a shelter for homeless women.

PHOTO BY CLARE WINSLOW

She has taught poetry writing as a volunteer at a shelter for women, and edited a collection of their poetry, Heart of the Oasis.

Based on her work, she has received a residency grant at the Vermont Studio Center as well as a writer's grant and three Larry Neal Awards for Poetry from the DC Commission on the Arts & Humanities. With her husband, John, a visual artist, she divides her time between downtown Washington, DC, and rural New Hampshire.

About the Artist

JOHN WINSLOW is a Washington, DC-based figurative painter. The recipient of awards from the Louis Comfort Tiffany Foundation and the DC Commission on the Arts & Humanities, he has exhibited paintings at the American Academy of Arts and Letters, the San Francisco Museum of Modern Art, the Brooklyn Museum, the Philadelphia Museum of Art, the Carnegie Institute, and many others. A selection of the public institutions that own his work includes the Corcoran, the Metropolitan Opera at Lincoln Center, the Butler Institute of Art, the New Orleans Museum of Art, the Washington, DC Convention Center, the Katzen Museum of American University, and the John A. Wilson Building City Hall Art Collection of Washington DC. Visit www.johnwinslow.com.

ABOUT THE HILARY THAM CAPITAL COLLECTION

The HILARY THAM CAPITAL COLLECTION (HTC COLLECTION) is an imprint by The Word Works that features excellence in poetry from authors in the Greater Washington, DC area. The hallmark of this series is that each book selected is financially supported by advance book sales and community contributions. The author also agrees to work with the press to promote the Capital Collection books, support other activities of The Word Works, and increase public interest in poetry.

In 1989, Hilary Tham was the first author published in the Capital Collection imprint. In 1994 when she became Word Works Editor-in-Chief, she revitalized the imprint, which had produced only two titles. By June 2005, Ms. Tham had paved the way for publication of thirteen additional Capital Collection titles.

The following individuals and organizations have contributed to the Capital Collection to make this book possible:

PATRONS: J. H. Beall • Michele Gates • Joe Goldberg
Miles Moore • Michele Nunemacher
Harriet & David Plant • Pamela Ward

DONORS: Rich & Jan Haswell • Kimm & Ray Jolly • Judith
McCombs • Chele Miller • Mary Morrison • Joyce
Neff • Mary W. Poole • Leila Sachenik • Joseph
Sendry • Jean Sinclair Symmes • Elizabeth Solomon
Mick Souter • Barbara Stout • Joan Weber
Patricia Thomas & Lauren Welch

FRIENDS: Karren Alenier • Paul Grayson • Maxine Kern
Jack & Ariel Leibowitz • Barbara Sobol

Thanks also to our generous anonymous donors.

ABOUT THE WORD WORKS

THE WORD WORKS, a nonprofit literary organization, publishes contemporary poetry in collectors' editions. Since 1981, the organization has sponsored the Washington Prize, a $1,500 award to an American poet. Monthly, The Word Works presents free literary programs in the Chevy Chase Café Muse series, and each summer, free poetry programs are held at the historic Joaquin Miller Cabin in Washington, DC's Rock Creek Park. Annually, two high school students debut in the Miller Cabin Series as winners of the Jacklyn Potter Young Poets Competition.

Since 1974, WORD WORKS programs have included: "In the Shadow of the Capitol," a symposium and archival project on the African-American intellectual community in segregated Washington, DC; the Gunston Arts Center Poetry Series (Ai, Carolyn Forché, Stanley Kunitz, and others); the Poet-Editor panel discussions at the Bethesda Writer's Center (John Hollander, Maurice English, Anthony Hecht, Josephine Jacobsen, and others); and the Arts Retreat in Tuscany. Master Class workshops, an ongoing program, have featured Agha Shahid Ali, Thomas Lux, and Marilyn Nelson.

In 2007, THE WORD WORKS will have published 64 titles, including work from such authors as Deirdra Baldwin, J.H. Beall, Christopher Bursk, John Pauker, Edward Weismiller, and Mac Wellman. Currently, THE WORD WORKS publishes books and occasional anthologies under three imprints: the Washington Prize, the Hilary Tham Capital Collection, and International Editions.

Past grants have been awarded by the National Endowment for the Arts, National Endowment for the Humanities, DC Commission on the Arts & Humanities, Witter Bynner Foundation, Writer's Center, Bell Atlantic, Batir Foundation, and others, including many generous private patrons.

THE WORD WORKS has established an archive of artistic and administrative materials in the Washington Writing Archive housed in the George Washington University Gelman Library.

Please enclose a self-addressed, stamped envelope with all inquiries.

The Word Works   PO Box 42164   Washington, DC 20015
editor@wordworksdc.com   www.wordworksdc.com

OTHER WORD WORKS BOOKS

Karren L. Alenier, Hilary Tham, Miles David Moore, EDS.,
   Winners: A Retrospective of the Washington Prize
* Nathalie F. Anderson, *Following Fred Astaire*
* Michael Atkinson, *One Hundred Children Waiting for a Train*
Mel Belin, *Flesh That Was Chrysalis* (HTC COLLECTION)
* Carrie Bennett, *biography of water*
* Peter Blair, *Last Heat*
Doris Brody, *Judging the Distance* (HTC COLLECTION)
Sarah Browning, *Whiskey in the Garden of Eden* (HTC COLLECTION)
Christopher Conlon, *Gilbert and Garbo in Love*
   (HTC COLLECTION)
Christopher Conlon, *Mary Falls* (HTC COLLECTION)
Donna Denizé, *Broken Like Job* (HTC COLLECTION)
Moshe Dor, Barbara Goldberg, Giora Leshem, EDS.,
   The Stones Remember
James C. Hopkins, *Eight Pale Women* (HTC COLLECTION)
James C. Hopkins & Yoko Danno, *The Blue Door*
   (INTERNATIONAL EDITIONS)
Brandon D. Johnson, *Love's Skin* (HTC COLLECTION)
Myong-Hee Kim, *Crow's Eye View: The Infamy of Lee Sang,*
   Korean Poet (INTERNATIONAL EDITIONS)
Vladimir Levchev, *Black Book of the Endangered Species*
   (INTERNATIONAL EDITIONS)
* Richard Lyons, *Fleur Carnivore*
* Fred Marchant, *Tipping Point*
Judith McCombs, *The Habit of Fire* (HTC COLLECTION)
* Ron Mohring, *Survivable World*
Miles David Moore, *The Bears of Paris* (HTC COLLECTION)
Miles David Moore, *Rollercoaster* (HTC COLLECTION)
Jacklyn Potter, Dwaine Rieves, Gary Stein, EDS.
   Cabin Fever: Poets at Joaquin Miller's Cabin
* Jay Rogoff, *The Cutoff*
Robert Sargent, *Aspects of a Southern Story*
Robert Sargent, *A Woman From Memphis*
* Enid Shomer, *Stalking the Florida Panther*
* John Surowiecki, *The Hat City After Men Stopped Wearing Hats*
Maria Terrone, *The Bodies We Were Loaned* (HTC COLLECTION)
Hilary Tham, *Bad Names for Women* (HTC COLLECTION)
Hilary Tham, *Counting* (HTC COLLECTION)
Jonathan Vaile, *Blue Cowboy* (HTC COLLECTION)
* Miles Waggener, *Phoenix Suites*

   * WASHINGTON PRIZE WINNERS